Dopamine Detox

Avoid Distractions, Stop Wasting Time on the Internet, and Take Back Control Over Your Life

Gary Miles

© 2022 Gary Miles. All rights reserved.

The content within this book may not be reproduced, duplicated, or transmitted without direct written permission from the author and/or the publisher.

Under no circumstances will any blame or legal responsibility be held against the publisher and/or author, for any damages, reparation, or monetary loss due to the information contained within this book, either directly or indirectly.

Legal Notice

This book is copyright protected. It is for personal use only. You cannot amend, distribute, sell, use, or paraphrase any part, or the content within this book, without the consent of the author and/or publisher.

Disclaimer Notice

Please note that the information contained within this document is for educational and entertainment purposes only. All effort has been executed to present accurate, up-to-date, reliable, and complete information. No warranties of any kind are declared or implied. Readers acknowledge that the author is not rendering legal, financial, medical, or professional advice.

Table of Contents

Table of Contents 3

Introduction 4

Chapter 1: Dopamine Addictions 6

Chapter 2: Dopamine and Instant Gratification 17

Chapter 3: Activities to Engage In 21

Chapter 4: Dopamine and Food 29

Chapter 5: Pomodoro Technique in Dopamine Detox 45

Chapter 6: Taking Control of Your Dopamine 49

Chapter 7: The Dopamine Detox 55

Chapter 8: Dopamine Reset 75

Chapter 9: Why Bad Habits are Hard to Break? 79

Chapter 10: Phone Addiction 81

Chapter 11: Establishing New Habits 89

Chapter 12: Ways to Naturally Boost Dopamine 93

Chapter 13: Controlling Your Dopamine for Motivation, Focus, and Satisfaction 97

Chapter 14: Proven Ways to STOP Being Lazy 105

Chapter 15: How to Make Hard Work SUPER EASY 108

Conclusion 112

Author's Note 114

Introduction

Are you someone who feels constantly busy but never gets enough done? Do you find yourself frequently fighting the urge to check your phone for notifications during work hours but end up giving in to the impulse?

The problem is that you had a feeling that you probably won't find any notifications - but you still went ahead and checked your phone. Unfortunately, it doesn't feel as good as you anticipated it to be - not that it stops you from waiting for the next notification.

Now, replace waiting for notifications with any other behavior you feel you've become too hooked on. It can be eating sugar or junk food, watching porn, shopping, smoking, playing video games, or drinking coffee - basically, any behavior you feel is taking up too much of your time, focus, and anticipation. It's affecting your life so much that it's interfering with your productivity and success.

In hindsight, you probably know how fruitless and draining this behavior is, although it feels like it's out of your hands.

The truth you may be denying and struggling to accept is that you've become a borderline addict to the behavior.

Do you remember the days when you were so focused and driven that you'd always be the hardest worker in the room? Do you miss the days when you were so productive that the word "procrastination" had no meaning in your dictionary? If that's the case, I'm confident this book is exactly what you need at this point in your life.

It has been written to help you understand the root cause of all your problems, which is none other than dopamine - a neurotransmitter secreted by our brains. It may sound a little complicated initially, but that's why I've created this book for you.

I'll help you understand the role dopamine plays in driving our desires and then take it a step further to help you realize, understand, and overcome your addictions. I'll shed light on the most common dopamine-addictive activities, ranging from eating sugar to video gaming to watching pornography or even just using your smartphone.

Once you know how chasing the dopamine high affects your life, we'll trek through all the dopamine fasting and diets designed to reset your dopamine levels. You may be skeptical at first, but you'll soon embrace the magic of a dopamine detox once you've confirmed its efficacy.

Chapter 1:
Dopamine Addictions

In this chapter of the book, we'll learn more about dopamine, where it comes from, how it's distributed around our bodies, and what kind of behavioral and lifestyle factors help boost the production of nature's happy hormone.

What is Dopamine?

Despite what some may believe, happiness is indeed within us. The human brain is a fascinating thing. It can make you feel everything or if it chooses to, nothing. All of our physical and emotional feelings are made in our heads and distributed throughout our bodies.

Questions such as what dopamine does and how it even does it, have been controversial in the neuroscience industry for decades. More than 110,000 studies have been released about dopamine but it remains to be a controversial topic among scientists. Dopamine is a neurotransmitter. This neurotransmitter helps us feel all of our emotions and helps us control and regulate our movement. It even helps with our attention span and learning. One of the things it's responsible for is sending signals between our nerve cells.

Chemical messengers in the brain are called neurotransmitters. These messengers are attached to molecules called receptors. These so-called receptors' job is to move the neurotransmitter that's carrying the signal from one cell to another. Very few neurons make dopamine and not every transmitter is made in the same part of the brain either. All of these brain areas might be tiny but they're solely responsible for our dopamine needs.

- The substantia nigra area: Dopamine produced from the substantia nigra area helps to initiate movements and speech.
- The ventral tegmental area aka VTA: The functions of dopamine produced in this part of the brain are less well defined and are the main source of controversy among neuroscientists. Dopamine that's produced in the VTA doesn't directly help people move or do things. What it does is that it sends dopamine to the brain when we expect a reward. It could be the actual simplest thing like your favorite food or a good classic song from your teen years. Not all neurons in the actual VTA produce dopamine. Many studies suggest that the

sudden appearance of unwanted or harmful stimuli, such as pain, causes the activation of certain neurons in the ventral tegmental area.
- Finally, the pyriform complex of the olfactory bulb is responsible for providing humans with a sense of smell. In the mesolimbic pathway, dopamine is released in pleasurable situations. It causes arousal and motivates behavior for pleasurable activity or pursuit. Here, it binds to dopaminergic receptors and transmits signals. Thus, it takes part in the following roles:
  - Situation assessment and analysis function
  - Engine control mechanism
  - Motivation
  - Behavior reinforcement
  - Reward mechanism

The functions of dopamine in our body are too many to count. Dopamine is decisive in almost all the functions of the brain and is the main motivator behind our actions and relationships.

Below are the most basic functions of dopamine.

Dopamine and Mobility

The basal ganglia are responsible for all of our brain-controlled movements. But, if we want our basal ganglia to work without problems, the neighboring neurons have to release a lot of dopamine.

Excessive production of dopamine can cause the body some problems as well. For example, too much dopamine can cause you to make unnecessary movements. It's a little-known fact that the main reason for the uncontrollable repetitive movements known as 'tics' is the excessive production of dopamine by neurons.

Sometimes the cells that make our dopamine supply die unexpectedly. Surprisingly, scientists still don't know why that happens. Researchers are currently investigating the role genetics play, the environmental factors, and the natural aging process in cell death and Parkinson's disease; a disease where one has uncontrollable hand tremors. It can occur in men and women around the age of 60. Some people develop Parkinson's disease as early as 40.

The Effect of Dopamine on Memory and Learning

The prefrontal cortex, which is involved in thinking and memory, is often associated with dopamine. Even minor fluctuations in the amount of dopamine in the prefrontal cortex can directly and significantly affect memory. In addition to the learning processes, dopamine also has an effect on which and how information is stored.

Dopamine helps us remember happy memories that spark joy better than not-so-happy ones. You can also get your prefrontal cortex to produce some dopamine when you participate in your favorite activity.

The Effect of Dopamine on Attention and Focus

Dopamine works by responding to the optic nerves, which allow you to focus on a certain subject or thing. A lack of dopamine and low dopamine concentration in the prefrontal cortex can cause you to have trouble paying attention and focusing.

How Dopamine Affects Perception

Dopamine determines how we perceive our experiences and events. Dopamine, which is released when we are having a pleasant time, makes us want to do this pleasant activity again in the future. For example, dopamine is the reason why we want to eat our favorite foods again and get pleasure from sexual intercourse. In short, dopamine allows us to take pleasure from our actions, just like the hormone serotonin.

Dopamine, Stress, and Excitement

Dopamine is also produced in high amounts when we encounter situations and events that excite us or cause sudden stress.

Effect of Dopamine on Mood

Dopamine releases feelings of pleasure and decides our mood. Why we enjoy some events and hate others can be explained by our internal production and release of dopamine from the brain areas mentioned previously. Dopamine is often called the "happy" hormone and a lack of it can trigger depression.

Effect of Dopamine on Sleep Patterns

Dopamine, which is released more during the day, is produced in lesser amounts late in the evening. That contributes to the natural sleep-wake cycle and causes drowsiness near the end of the day. The reason why Parkinson's patients tend to sleep a lot is the insufficient secretion of dopamine. Patients with psychosis, neurosis, and schizophrenia, in whom dopamine is over-produced, also tend to sleep a lot.

Signs of Dopamine Deficiency

There are multiple signs of dopamine deficiency, and they'll be listed here for easy reference. Keep in mind, this particular list is not meant to replace the proper diagnosis of a medical professional. The signs of dopamine deficiency are:

- Tremors and loss of balance
- Weight loss or weight gain
- Muscle cramps, spasms, and stiffness
- Eating and swallowing difficulties
- Unfocused and low energy
- Feeling tired and sluggish
- Unexplained sadness
- Moving slower than usual
- Hopelessness, suicidal thoughts, and feelings of guilt
- Hallucinating
- Lack of self-awareness
- Worry and anxiety

Dopamine deficiency can have multiple causes. These causes are often related to mental health disorders. Drug use, an unhealthy diet, and consumption of foods high in sugar and saturated fat can also lead to this deficiency. Due to the lack of dopamine, many health problems can develop in us.

Diseases Caused by Dopamine Deficiency

Dopamine deficiency causes multiple disorders. Each disorder is characterized by a slightly different version of the deficiency. The following diseases are characterized by some form of dopamine deficiency:

- Social phobia and psychosis
- Depression
- ADHD
- Insomnia and anhedonia
- Parkinson's disease

In Parkinson's, dopamine deficiency is well described by the brain's inability to produce dopamine due to the death of dopamine-producing cells in the substantia nigra. Parkinson's disease shows its first symptoms in the form of tremors in the fingers and hands. The disease is further accompanied by symptoms such as excessive sweating, weight loss, and depressed mood.

Dopamine and Mental Health

In addition to dopamine deficiency, excessive secretion of dopamine can also trigger mental problems. For example, it's known that dopamine is produced excessively in the brains of schizophrenic and bipolar patients. In addition, the person may experience an extremely cheerful mood, high blood pressure, and accelerated heartbeat. The patient may experience results such as hyperactivity, paranoia, stress, restlessness, insomnia, tension, anxiety, and inattention.

Dopamine Provides Pleasure

Dopamine also affects mood. Dopamine is what drives a lab animal to press a lever repeatedly, for example, to get tasty food. This is why people want to eat another slice of pizza; the taste has a rewarding response from our brains. Reward and reinforcement both help us learn where we can find important things like food and water so that more can be obtained. Surviving a negative event can also be considered a reward. Without dopamine, or with lower amounts of it, you wouldn't be able to enjoy things as simple as eating and drinking as much as you would have with regular dopamine production. This goes for both humans and other animals; less dopamine generally results in less pleasure. There's a name for this unpleasant state. It's called anhedonia, or the loss of pleasure.

Addiction and Dopamine

What drug addiction and Parkinson's disease have in common is insufficient dopamine levels. People who produce smaller amounts of dopamine may be prone to addiction more than those who don't. A specific dopamine receptor and its presence in our brains can be associated with seeking sensations and taking risks.

Most importantly, it affects mental health and enjoyment, increases motivation, and makes the person happy. The use of alcohol, cocaine, stimulants such as nicotine, and other substances like heroin increase dopamine production. This increase forces people to seek these addictive substances again and again, even if they're fatally harmful.

Short-term use of chemical drugs also produces the same reward and pleasure for almost all humans. What is okay about that is that things quickly go back to the way they were. However, exposure to drugs can desensitize us to them over time and make us way more tolerant of the drug than we should be.

The person now needs even more of the drug to get the same positive emotions that once occurred naturally, which is the reason the drug was taken in the first place. Long-term excessive drug or alcohol use hijacks the brain, controlling emotions, motivation, and mood.

Addiction Treatment

The treatment of substance addiction varies according to the characteristics of the addictive substance and individuals. Substance addiction treatment can be done in three ways;

- Normal treatment
- In-patient treatment at a treatment center
- Prevention therapy

Dopamine function can be restored to its normal state with the help of psychotherapy, medications, and other treatments. This may take some time, depending on the substance used, and the duration of use. It's always recommended to work with a trained medical addiction specialist, rather than trying to heal alone but there are some things you can do to kick-start your healing process. We'll get to that in just a little bit.

Safe and effective remediation is possible. Long-term or excessive use of drugs and alcohol can irreversibly alter brain structures and behavior. However, with treatment, the addicted person can learn how to live with brain and behavioral changes. Plenty of recovering addicts live a great life post-addiction thanks to their treatments but unfortunately, addiction can't be cured completely.

Chapter 2:
Dopamine and Instant Gratification

Dopamine is a neurotransmitter that drives our desire to seek out pleasure. It also fuels impulsive behavior and can lead to addiction

Dopamine acts as the primary reinforcement signal in the brain. This means that when an animal finds an unexpected reward, the dopamine neurons in the brain release a burst of dopamine. This makes the animal seek out the reward again, and eventually, this process teaches the animal the correct way to behave in the world.

Dopamine is important for motor control and mood regulation, and also plays important roles in the immune system, the gastrointestinal tract, and the pancreas. It's also responsible for regulating blood flow and inhibiting norepinephrine. It plays a vital role in memory, mood, and cognition.

Dopamine is also involved in several addictive behaviors. For example, compulsive behavior can lead to a rush of dopamine in the brain and can make a person feel like they are losing control of their behavior. Furthermore, dopamine has been found in the brains of schizophrenia patients. This may be responsible for some of the positive symptoms of the disorder.

It Drives Us to Seek Pleasure

When you have a pleasurable experience, note any cues that occur in the environment that remind you of that experience, and your brain will release dopamine in response. This can create a powerful urge to repeat the experience. In many cases, this drive for pleasure doesn't involve using harmful substances.

Dopamine also plays an important role in motivation and movement. But its association with pleasure is sometimes misunderstood. For example, animal studies have found that dopamine levels are closely associated with the urge to perform a certain activity, not with the actual enjoyment the activity brings. Instead, a new theory suggests that dopamine helps the brain predict whether or not an experience will be pleasant and rewarding. When the experience exceeds expectations, dopamine levels are higher, indicating that we'll experience more pleasure.

Dopamine is critical in addiction. When we ingest drugs that alter our dopamine levels, our reward system will shift in a way that makes it easier to engage in addictive behaviors. This means that addictive behavior will take precedence and our motivation will shift accordingly. For example, when we eat a delicious meal, we feel a flood of dopamine. We also experience a rush of dopamine when we find a $20 bill on the floor. However, experts are still investigating how dopamine plays a role in addiction.

It Fuels Impulsive Behavior

In an attempt to understand the underlying mechanisms behind impulsive behavior, researchers have discovered that dopamine plays a pivotal role.

It Can Lead to Addiction

Dopamine is one of the most widely used drugs in the world and is commonly referred to as the "feel-good" hormone. Its molecular structure resembles that of an insect with long antennae. It has become a popular tattoo design. In addition to its role in addiction, dopamine also affects the brain's calculating and emotion-related systems.

Drugs can cause severe impairments in the brain, affecting the areas responsible for reward, pain relief, learning, memory, and emotional regulation. The effects of addiction can persist for years after a person stops using substances. This is because addiction rewires the brain to expect instant gratification.

It Can Lead to Overindulgence

Dopamine and instant gratification are powerful brain chemicals that cause us to indulge. But the negatives of overindulgence outweigh the benefits.

Overindulging makes us feel better in the moment, but over time, we crave more. Our pleasure threshold increases over time, and the next time we crave the same thing, we'll feel less pleasure. This spirals out of control. If you're worried about overindulgence, try to plan your indulgence ahead of time.

While instant gratification is controlled by the limbic system, delayed gratification is controlled by the prefrontal cortex. Delaying gratification can help you avoid overindulgence by teaching yourself to enjoy your reward after a period of waiting. You can start practicing delayed gratification by enjoying small portions of your favorite treat after eating dinner, or even after completing chores.

Chapter 3:
Activities to Engage In

During the detox, your brain usually rewires itself to not depend on one (or two) activities to feel happy. Your happiness and aptitude for pleasure return to normal or baseline levels. This exercise is also meant to show you that you control your behaviors; you don't have to look at a bottle and drink it if you don't want to. You don't have to play a video game just because you don't want to do anything else. You don't have to be triggered by external events. You hold all the power.

Yes, you'll still remember what it was like to feel exhilarated while watching those porn videos. Dopamine plays a big role in how we remember things, and if we aren't careful, we can fall back into old habits of excessive porn and masturbation, of buying unnecessary things although we still have bills to pay. That's why if you can't moderate your behavior when engaging in that activity, like only going on a shopping spree once every two months instead of weekly, then maybe you should pay off and close your credit card. Put debit orders in place to ensure your money goes to the right channels before spending. Perhaps get an accountability partner who'll check in on you and you can talk to every time you feel like your life is spiraling.

Another great option is to find replacement habits for the activities you're addicted to, something you can do instead when you get triggered. Now, you mustn't find replacements while you're detoxing. During the detox, your mind is meant to be clear and free from any dopamine-inducing or replacing behaviors. You want to be still for hours, thinking, reflecting, and perhaps journaling. Once you're through the detox, you can consider a replacement like giving a dollar to charity every time you think of spending, reading a book instead of tweets, learning to play chess instead of video games, or eating fruit instead of cookies.

Another great replacement for just about all the behaviors I've described as toxic is exercise. Remember that exercise only feels good if you enjoy it, so find something to do that will help you move your body, whether it's dancing, yoga, or cycling. Exercising is a great option because you can't do much while exercising, so it'll be easy to keep your mind distracted, in a more positive way.

Remember that you have choices when you get the urge to engage in any toxic activity you've listed while detoxing. You can practice mindfulness and stay on top of your thoughts before they spiral completely out of control. You can meditate, listen to positive music, or watch a positive documentary to break away from the negative toxic cycle your brain may have fallen into. You can exercise, talk to a friend or a counselor, do some physical labor like cleaning the house or yard, play with your pet, or become reacquainted with people you haven't spoken to in a while. You can call someone on the phone, write someone a letter, or go for a long drive. You can volunteer.

This is your chance to be mindful, to focus on what is important to you, and to meditate on questionnaires like the *What Matters Most Now*. You can do important things - something with meaning or purpose. You can share positive messages with people on social networks or anonymously. You can stay off those dopamine-driven platforms for a week or two, helping you get back to reality, to your life and your passions, to things that are purely motivating because they are rewarding.

After your dopamine detox, you'll feel your life is less complicated, more satisfying, and quieter - a time in your life when you feel you have more control over your thoughts, emotions, and behaviors. Your life will feel more meaningful. You'll not look at that bottle of wine or pills since they're no longer your answers. Your life will be simple and balanced, with less stress, less fear, less anxiety, and more freedom.

Mindfulness

Another practice that helps keep us present is being mindful of our habits and thoughts. When you're constantly seeking out dopamine you often do so unconsciously, and you're hardly fully present while you're engaging in those activities. Like watching TV and putting food in your mouth; the next thing you know, your plate is empty, and you think about how long you have to wait before it's appropriate to eat a snack. When you stop layering dopamine-inducing activities on top of each other you're more likely to be mindful of the activities themselves. You'll get to taste the different flavors in the food you're eating, and learn to enjoy food, for the sake of food, not because it's something to do as you scroll through social media.

Mindfulness can also be practiced by taking a moment to enjoy your life. Look around you, is your family blessed and healthy? Do you have all your basic needs covered? Being aware of these, and grateful for them, goes a long way in keeping us happy. If you like, you can even take a walk around a park, go hiking along a safe forest trail or take a drive to the beach. There's so much beauty in nature that we've come to miss because we're so focused on ourselves, what we should get or how we should feel, that we don't see that we already have so much.

Meditation

Meditation is a great practice for becoming more aligned with the present and has been known to keep anxiety at bay. Because the goal of meditation is to focus on your breathing and your body, you get to keep your mind clear of any troubling thoughts. If you'd like to learn more about meditation, I strongly suggest you check out the work of Dr. Joe Dispenza, a neuroscientist who believed in the power of the mind to cultivate the life we desire and has helped thousands of people do just that. I'd like to share two of his meditation practices with you, found in his book, *Becoming Supernatural*. The meditation practices Dispenza shares in his book have helped his clients achieve unbelievable results from lowering cancer markers, to creating new jobs, from finding love to winning the lottery. Whatever you want is within your grasp.

Do this for at least 10 minutes a day (preferably in the morning), but throughout the day, set two to four reminders where you practice feeling those emotions. With your mental energy focused on positive feelings, it'll be difficult to feel the opposite, and transition back to those emotions that had you dependent on dopamine to sustain your life.

The Walking Meditation

Start your practice out in nature: the park, hiking trail, or on the beach. Focus your attention on your chest, heart, and the external space around them.

After about 10 minutes of walking, stop and turn around. Bringing up those feelings you want for your future, and truly embodying them as you send those emotions through your body and the space around it. After about two to three minutes, open your eyes and begin walking back. At the end of your practice, you should affirm the feeling that's showing up in your body and mind at this very moment, so you can say something like: "I am powerful." If there are people around you, maybe even staring, you'll eventually learn to ignore them completely.

More to Consider

Cold Water Submersion

Taking cold showers, or dunking one's body in cold water (up to the neck) is a technique that has become popularized by the likes of Wim Hof (also known as The Iceman), but has been around for decades. Huberman explains that when you do cold water submersion for at least five minutes. So, your reflex will tell you to get out of the water or turn on the hot water nozzle, but try to stay calm. You can distract yourself by singing, chanting some positive affirmations, and breathing in and out slowly and deeply while focusing on the elevated feeling you want to embody.

People have reported feeling a weird but amazing mixture of calm and alertness after the exposure. Dopamine levels have been tracked to increase 250% above baseline, and unlike other activities that have a quick dip, after cold water exposure, dopamine levels are sustained for a couple of hours, and some have reported the dip to not feel as extreme. This may be because adrenalin also contributes to the increase and it isn't known to have a dip. At some point, your body will become adapted to the cold water. You can try colder water, but nothing below 40 degrees Fahrenheit. Like every other dopamine activity, simply detox for a couple of weeks.

Enough sleep

Getting enough sleep at the right times is important. Most people are cranky after sleeping late, or not getting sufficient sleep throughout the night. A study conducted by Romeo, et al., revealed that being exposed to bright lights at night (between 10 p.m. and 4 a.m.) would "oxidize dopamine and, in turn, induce the formation of neuromelanin, and cause dopamine neuron degeneration" (Romeo et al., 2013). If you have to stay up after 10 p.m. (putting in a few extra hours of work, not watching more series), you can use blue-light-blocking glasses in the evenings, use candles instead of a light bulb, and decrease the brightness levels of your PC.

On a related but slightly different topic, melatonin, which is the natural hormone related to your sleep-wake cycles, causes a decrease in dopamine. This makes sense because dopamine is meant to keep you alert and focused, it only makes sense that to get sufficient rest, there's a counter hormone. The problem is some people who struggle to fall asleep take supplements with melatonin which decreases dopamine levels beyond sleep, affecting their mood even when they're awake. There are other, more practical ways, to fall asleep quicker like lowering the temperature in your home, meditation, and yoga, not taking naps during the day, and eating better.

Meaningful Relationships

Social media has kept us connected without having to connect. Although it has its benefits, it's more beneficial for our dopamine and overall well-being if we foster real-life romantic relationships and friendships, or connect with our kids (for the parents out there).

Chapter 4:
Dopamine and Food

What you put into your body directly impacts your dopamine levels. Eat foods high in protein and healthy fats, like nuts and seeds. Avoid processed foods and sugary snacks. Eat plenty of fruits and vegetables, especially leafy greens. Drink plenty of water and avoid caffeine and alcohol. When you eat healthy foods, you're giving your body the nutrients needed to produce dopamine.

You might want to consider cutting out completely, all highly-processed foods. Not only are they bad for dopamine, but they are also harmful to your gut microbiome. Highly-processed foods have been designed to taste extremely good and increase your dopamine levels extensively, making you crave more junk food and less of the wholesome foods that are good for you. After just a few days of detoxing processed foods, even the blandest foods, like cauliflower, start to taste reasonably good - especially when sprinkled with parmesan cheese.

Whole foods like chicken, salmon, eggs, spinach, yogurt, nuts, and seeds are good for your gut microbiome. A healthy gut microbiome has been shown to improve one's overall mood. According to Strandwitz, studies around the gut-brain pathways show that the microbiome consumes and produces the neurotransmitters dopamine, serotonin, and gamma-aminobutyric acid (GABA). Much like many other neurotransmitters, GABA has a wide range of functions. Still, the one that's important for the context of this book is its ability to inhibit feelings of stress and promote feelings of relaxation and calmness., eating the right foods could potentially increase your dopamine levels to natural levels (especially if it's been depleted) while improving your overall mood and temperament.

You can try some over-the-counter supplements to help you increase your dopamine levels. Huberman explains that supplements aren't as addictive as other activities I've highlighted. Still, just like those activities, you'll find that after the dopamine peak, you'll be met with an equally powerful dip.

Common Supplements

Mucuna pruriens: These can be found in the form of beans (sometimes called velvety beans) and in capsule form. Mucuna pruriens are rich in L-dopa, a molecule that gets turned into dopamine within the brain. Other great benefits are that they can reduce symptoms of Parkinson's disease and increase sperm count.

L-tyrosine: This is a nonessential amino acid that gets turned into L-dopa. The capsule form of L-tyrosine has been shown to help people become more alert and focused. Still, they're not good for people who suffer from anxiety, so always consult a medical practitioner before getting these.

Huperzine-A: This chemical increases dopamine, particularly in your prefrontal cortex and hippocampus, leading to improved critical thinking and memory.

On top of using the right foods, you can do other easy things to keep your dopamine levels in check. Stay active for at least 30 minutes of moderate to vigorous aerobic exercise or 20 minutes of yoga. Engage in new activities, or do new types of things, like traveling to a new country and eating cultural dishes, doing new exercises at the gym, playing a new sport, or taking on a new hobby that's out of your comfort zone.

The key to feeding your brain dopamine is to feed it the right foods and activities while also taking a few steps to decrease the amount of dopamine your brain has already built up.

What is Dopamine Fasting?

Addiction to certain foods can be just as powerful as addiction to drugs or alcohol. Sugar, salt, and processed foods are all common culprits. While it's not always easy to break the addiction, dopamine fasting may provide a way to do just that.

Dopamine fasting is designed to help you break your addiction to it. It involves limiting the number of things that stimulate dopamine release. This practice can also involve periods without technology, social media, sex, or food.

Dopamine fasting can help decrease the brain's dependence on external sources to get its "fix." It can increase your ability to generate dopamine through internal sources, as well as boost your ability to regulate dopamine levels yourself. It has also been known to increase motivation, creativity, empathy, and a general outlook on life.

For most people, the idea of a "dopamine fast" sounds like something that could only be achieved by a monk who has spent a lifetime trying to quiet their mind. But in fact, our brains are constantly releasing dopamine, the chemical that gives us feelings of pleasure and motivation.

You might think that's not a bad thing, but according to some researchers, we're living in an age where we're constantly bombarded with pleasurable stimuli. This causes many people to crave these things more often or in greater quantity than they should. This inevitably can lead to problems such as obesity and addiction.

You can't stop your brain from releasing dopamine, but the concept of fasting is about restricting the things that cause it to be released so you can regain your sensitivity to those things. There's nothing wrong with enjoying these things in moderation, but when they become a crutch, they can be difficult to break free from. That's where dopamine fasting comes in.

How to Adjust Nutrition for Dopamine Fasting

There is no one perfect diet for dopamine fasting. However, you can do a few general things to adjust your nutrition and make the experience more beneficial.

Reduce Your Intake of Sugar, Processed Foods, and Caffeine

Processed foods, sugar, and caffeine are all known to stimulate dopamine release. Try to reduce your intake of these things while fasting. Always check the ingredients list on food labels and avoid anything with sugar, high fructose corn syrup, or artificial sweeteners. The same goes for caffeine. Try to avoid coffee, tea, and energy drinks while dopamine fasting. It helps to have a plan for what you will eat instead of these things.

Eat More Whole Foods

Whole foods are less processed and contain more nutrients than processed foods. They also tend to have a lower glycemic index, meaning they won't cause blood sugar spikes. Try to make at least 50% of your diet whole foods by including things like fruits, vegetables, whole grains, and lean proteins. You can also try to eat mindfully by paying attention to how you're feeling after eating different foods. If you feel good after eating a certain food, it's likely a good choice for dopamine fasting.

Drink Plenty of Fluids

Fluids are important because they help to flush toxins from the body. Try to drink plenty of water, herbal teas, and detox drinks. Avoid caffeine and alcohol, as they dehydrate your body. It's also essential to get plenty of electrolytes, especially if you're exercising regularly.

Avoid Foods That Cause Intolerance or Allergy

Certain foods can cause inflammation in the body and lead to problems such as gas, bloating, and diarrhea. If you find that you have a food intolerance or allergy, avoid those foods while dopamine fasting. Fast-food restaurants are a common source of these foods. Burgers, fries, and pizza are all high in fat, sugar, and salt. They're also loaded with chemicals that can trigger inflammation.

Supplement with Omega-3s

Omega-3 fatty acids are important for overall health and can help reduce inflammation. They're especially beneficial for people who are on dopamine fast. Try to supplement with a quality omega-3 supplement. Foods high in omega-3s include salmon, walnuts, chia seeds, and flaxseeds. Other good sources of omega-3s include fish oil supplements and algae supplements.

Take a Probiotic

A probiotic is a good way to support gut health while dopamine fasting. The gut is home to trillions of bacteria, some of which are beneficial and some are not. Probiotics help to maintain a healthy balance of bacteria in the gut. They can also help reduce inflammation and improve digestion. Look for a probiotic that contains multiple strains of bacteria.

Avoid Foods That Are High in Lectins

Lectins are proteins found in many plant foods. They can cause inflammation and digestive problems. Foods that are high in lectins should be avoided while dopamine fasting. These foods include grains, legumes, and nightshade vegetables. Instead, focus on eating nutrient-rich fruits and vegetables.

Eat More Fermented Foods

Fermented foods are high in probiotics and can help support gut health. They're also a good source of the enzymes essential for digestion. Try to include fermented foods in your diet while dopamine fasting. Some good options include sauerkraut, kimchi, yogurt, and kefir.

Increase Your Intake of Healthy Fats

Healthy fats are essential for overall health. They help support the immune system, reduce inflammation, and improve brain function. While fasting, increase your intake of healthy fats by eating things like nuts, seeds, avocado, and olive oil. You can also drink smoothies made with healthy fats.

Avoid Eating Late at Night

Eating late at night can interfere with your sleep and sabotage your dopamine fasting efforts. Thoroughly chew all food to help with digestion. Make it a habit to eat slowly and mindfully, even when you're not fasting.

The Benefits of Dopamine Fasting

While dopamine fasting may seem like a new trend, there is some evidence to suggest that it can be beneficial for overall health. Below are some of the benefits that have been reported.

Improved Mental Clarity and Focus

One of the main benefits is improved mental clarity and focus. Dopamine fasting eliminates processed foods and unhealthy sugar from the diet. When the body is not bombarded with processed foods, it has a chance to reset and function more effectively. With only healthy, nutrient-rich foods being consumed, the mind focuses better and thinks more clearly.

Reduced Inflammation

Chronic inflammation is linked to several health problems, including heart disease, cancer, and arthritis. Reducing inflammation is essential for overall health. Dopamine fasting can help reduce inflammation due to the elimination of processed foods and the addition of healthy fats. The anti-inflammatory effects will be even greater if you take additional supplements while dopamine-fasting, such as fish oil or turmeric.

Weight Loss

This type of fast is also an effective way to lose weight. When you eliminate processed foods and focus on eating nutrient-rich foods, weight loss is inevitable. The best part of dopamine fasting is that it's a sustainable way to lose weight and keep it off. Eating this way is not a fad diet but a healthy, long-term way of eating.

Improved Mood

Processed foods are known to harm your mood. When you eliminate these foods and focus on eating healthy, nutrient-rich foods, your mood will improve. The body will no longer be in a state of toxicity and will be able to function at its best. You'll find that you have more energy and are less likely to experience mood swings.

Improved Digestion

Eating processed foods can wreak havoc on the digestive system. Your digestion will improve when you stop consuming these foods and focus on eating healthy, fiber-rich foods. By incorporating regular exercise into your dopamine fasting routine, you'll be on your way to optimal digestion. Sustained weight loss is also linked to better digestion.

Increased Energy Levels

Processed foods are high in sugar and caffeine, leading to a crash in energy levels. When you eliminate these foods and focus on eating healthy, nutrient-rich foods, your energy levels will increase. You'll find that you have more sustained energy throughout the day and are less likely to experience a mid-afternoon slump. Many people also report that they have more energy when they exercise while dopamine fasting.

Better Skin

Your skin is your body's largest organ, and it's vital to take care of it. Processed foods can harm skin health - inducing wrinkles, blemishes, and dryness. You will find that incorporating healthy, nutrient-rich foods into your diet will result in your skin being less oily, acne reduced, and wrinkles less noticeable.

Reduced Risk of Disease

Eating processed foods increases the risk of developing chronic diseases such as heart disease, cancer, and diabetes. Excess inflammation and the consumption of unhealthy sugar are to blame. Dopamine fasting can help reduce the risk of developing these diseases due to its anti-inflammatory effects and the focus on eating healthy, nutrient-rich foods.

Better Sleep

Processed foods can interfere with sleep quality and quantity. Irregular sleep patterns are linked to several health problems, including weight gain and an increased risk of disease. Healthy foods like those found in a dopamine-fasting diet help to promote good sleep habits. You'll find that you fall asleep more easily and sleep through the night without waking up.

Increased Lifespan

Studies have shown that a healthy diet can increase lifespan. Setting yourself up for a longer, healthier life requires eating nutrient-rich foods. Going on a dopamine fast is one way to do this. The benefits are vast and include improved mental clarity, reduced inflammation, weight loss, improved mood, and better digestion. It's worth giving it a try not only to get over addictive behavior but also to simply start living a healthier and better life.

Diets for Dopamine Fasting

Many different diets can be followed while dopamine fasting. Here are a few of the most popular ones:

Paleo Diet

The Paleo diet is based on the idea that humans are best suited to eat the same foods as our Paleolithic ancestors, meaning that processed foods, dairy, grains, and legumes are all off-limits. The Paleo diet focuses on eating a nutrient-rich diet with foods like fruits, vegetables, meat, poultry, seafood, and eggs. A few modifications can be made to the Paleo diet while dopamine fasting, such as avoiding starchy vegetables and consuming more healthy fats.

Mediterranean Diet

The Mediterranean diet is based on the traditional diet of countries bordering the Mediterranean Sea. It's high in fruits, vegetables, whole grains, legumes, fish, and healthy fats and low in meat and processed foods. The Mediterranean diet is a good option for dopamine fasting as it's nutrient-rich and allows for some flexibility in what you can eat. If you follow a vegetarian or vegan version of the Mediterranean diet, you can still reap its benefits while dopamine fasting.

Vegetarian Diet

A vegetarian diet eliminates all animal products, including meat, poultry, and seafood. There are many different types of vegetarian diets, but most focus on eating a variety of fruits, vegetables, whole grains, and legumes. A vegetarian diet can be followed while dopamine fasting with a few modifications, such as avoiding starchy vegetables and consuming more healthy fats. You may find you have more energy and better digestion when following a vegetarian diet while dopamine fasting.

Vegan Diet

Vegans consume only plant-based foods, eliminating all animal products, including meat, poultry, seafood, eggs, and dairy. Vegans may find it harder to stick to a healthy diet while dopamine fasting as fewer options are available. Try focusing on nutrient-rich foods like bananas, sweet potatoes, quinoa, and chia seeds.

Ketogenic Diet

The ketogenic diet is a high-fat, low-carbohydrate diet that helps to induce ketosis, a state in which the body uses fat for energy instead of carbohydrates. A ketogenic diet is a good option for dopamine fasting as it's very restrictive and limits the number of unhealthy foods that can be eaten. However, it can be difficult to follow and may not suit everyone.

Low-Carbohydrate Diet

A low-carbohydrate diet is a diet that restricts the number of carbohydrates eaten. Low-carbohydrate diets are popular for weight loss and are effective for dopamine fasting. There are many different types of low-carbohydrate diets, but most focus on eating a variety of healthy meats, vegetables, and fruits.

Macronutrient Diet

A macronutrient diet focuses on the ratio of macronutrients eaten, such as carbohydrates, proteins, and fats. A macronutrient diet can be followed while fasting, but make sure that the majority of your calories come from healthy sources like fruits, vegetables, and whole grains. Foods like candy and fast food should be avoided on this diet.

Intermittent Fasting

Intermittent fasting is an eating pattern where you eat during a specific time window and then fast for the rest of the day. Intermittent fasting can be followed while on a dopamine fast, but make sure you get the right nutrients during your feeding window.

Juice Fast

A juice fast is a type of fast where all the food eaten is juice. A juice fast can be followed while dopamine fasting if you include plenty of nutrient-rich fruits and vegetables in your juice recipes. It's a good way to detoxify your body and get a variety of nutrients. This diet is not recommended for people with a history of eating disorders.

Bone Broth Fast

A bone broth fast is a type of fast where t only bone broth is consumed. Bone broth is a good source of protein and other nutrients, making it a healthy choice for a fast. If you include plenty of vegetables in your recipes, it ensures you get the nutrients you need while dopamine fasting. Keto-adapted athletes often use bone broth fasts to increase ketone levels and improve athletic performance.

Chapter 5:
Pomodoro Technique in Dopamine Detox

The Pomodoro Technique is a popular time management tool that can help people focus on a single task at a time. It helps people stay focused on a task for 25 minutes at a time. You can learn how to use this technique in your everyday life to increase your productivity levels.

Focus on One Task at a Time

If you've struggled with motivation in the past, dopamine detox can help you restore focus by lowering your stimulation levels. In the first few days, a dopamine detox may seem difficult, as the body has to adjust to the lack of dopamine. Avoid binge-watching Netflix or listening to music. While these activities may seem enticing, they may not benefit your efforts. Long-form content is better for your brain. This is because it has lower chances of triggering compulsive behavior than short-form content. Remember, your brain is wired to seek out activities that produce the most dopamine.

Create an Uninterrupted Workflow Environment

Dopamine detox is a process that helps people sharpen their personalities. Many people engage in addictive behavior as a way to compensate for unmet emotional needs such as loneliness, anxiety, or anger. These behaviors often begin as a child or adolescent. When they experience one of these emotions, they often turn to another form of compensatory behavior, such as alcohol, drugs, or gambling.

Release Dopamine

Although the term "dopamine detox" is misleading, there are some real benefits to it. A dopamine detox allows you to unplug from pleasure and arousal-triggering activities for some time. This can help you focus better and achieve mental clarity.

The Pomodoro Technique is based on cognitive behavioral therapy (CBT), a well-established treatment for impulse disorders. The technique works by slowing the rate of gratification. In addition to improving productivity, the Pomodoro Technique helps with time management. Instead of gaming, try completing chores or taking a walk to avoid mindless scrolling.

While dopamine isn't directly responsible for pleasure, it's responsible for our feelings of reward.

The goal of a dopamine detox is to rewire the brain, and this will take time and effort. The key to success is to commit to the process.

Boost Productivity

To boost productivity, try using the Pomodoro Technique. This time-management technique helps employees stay focused and on task for short intervals of time. This technique is particularly effective for repetitive tasks. The Pomodoro interval is long enough to see progress in a task but short enough to not be monotonous.

It is important to maintain discipline when working towards long-term goals. For instance, students need to set study time and adhere to it. They must also avoid distractions and high-dopamine habits. For students, the Pomodoro Technique is an effective way to prioritize tasks and boost productivity.

Reduce Procrastination

The Pomodoro Technique helps people focus on a single task for a specified period. During this time, you can't be interrupted by urgent thoughts.

This method reduces procrastination by redefining a task as input rather than output. For example, writing a ten-page paper can be intimidating. However, with the

Pomodoro Technique, you can avoid procrastination by setting a timer to remind you of your time limit.

While this technique does not eliminate procrastination, it can help you create healthy habits. This technique helps you set realistic goals and manage failures effectively.

Chapter 6:
Taking Control of Your Dopamine

You're tired of how you invest energy.

You can't help yourself and quit surfing.

You need to make customary things fascinating and fun (and not have to have your telephone in your grasp continually to feel locked in).

The objectives are:

To break the example of urgent ways of behaving like browsing the web or getting your telephone without thinking. To acknowledge needing or hankering something doesn't mean we'll like it when we're getting it done. For instance, we may be overstating how it would feel to re-experience playing a specific game. In actuality, that's only our sentimentality at play.

Let the mind reestablish the dopamine receptors, so normal things become more fun.

The improved approach to defeating enslavement seems to be this:

Doing a dopamine detox is tied with following up on the longing to change and breaking the enthusiastic example. This gives you a space to move around, construct a superior life, and if you effectively attempt to do so, figure out how to deal with your feelings better.

What's the correct method for doing a dopamine detox?

How long would it be a good idea for you to do a dopamine detox?

By and large, 2-12 weeks. It requires investment for our cerebrums to rework.

14 days are the base to encounter recognizable impacts (that is why we made our test 14 days in length).

30 days are sufficiently long to see changes and make for a decent month-to-month challenge.

12 weeks is the average time skyline for internet fixation treatment (which is likewise near the well-known 90-day or 100-day challenges). This is most frequently to the point of changing your life, yet it tends to be too dismaying for many individuals.

Remove Exercises That Put You into Zombie Mode

Here is a guideline for you: For the span of the test, cut out things that make you go into Zombie Mode.

Remove Habit-forming Interruptions

Zombie Mode is the point at which you're simply looking over, watching, or playing for quite a long time, without truly getting a charge out of it, however unfit to stop and incapable of doing anything beneficial. It's the point at which you stall out for a long time taking part in modest dopamine exercises. The most widely recognized guilty parties are:

- Virtual entertainment
- Content aggregators (YouTube, Reddit, Hackernews)
- Marathon watching Netflix (binging)
- Computer games
- Pornography
- Possibly all of the above

You understand what your thing is. You could hear yourself legitimizing that you don't need to remove these exercises, that you will essentially control yourself a piece better, and it will be fine. You could give it a shot. Anyway, this is, in many cases, a reason because:

If you could direct your way of behaving, you wouldn't have the issue in the first place. Likewise, these exercises are often anchored together, so even though your central concern is YouTube, opening virtual entertainment frequently winds you up on YouTube.

Furthermore, with exhausted dopamine receptors, it's challenging to manage your way of behaving, and it's one of the objectives of the dopamine detox - to recapture the capacity to control your way of behaving.

Where to Track Down Inspiration for This

Your life may be wrecked. Or, on the other hand, you're doing well. However, you're not fulfilled and feel like you're burning through a ton of time. Another sign is if you have an issue stopping something like YouTube or computer games. That might be an indication that you truly need it.

Wanting to change is truly significant. If you're uncertain whether to do this, look at these justifications for why you quit surfing thoughtlessly.

Change can be hard, and we won't mislead you - it may be awkward for some time.

Nonetheless:

- It will be truly worth the effort.
- You can make it a lot simpler than you naturally suspect.

- You can constantly return to your past ways of behaving. This is NOT a Disney movie where everything turns out great.
- Acknowledge you're potential as of now, utilizing strategies to lessen the craving for computerized activities.

You might be concealing or undermining your routines because they must be your fixation - that you turned into a subordinate to them. Or you could have been doing it for quite a long time and may never know you did anything.

About the point of diminishing the craving and getting rid of the cell phone:

Don't just leave and start remarking, "I don't need this internet." That's too much work.

With practice, you can do this without an issue or with some assistance. Stay in moment-to-moment with the natural physical denial.

It will be truly demanding. You may have to quit time by time.

Don't beat yourself up if it comes to light.

If you did all you could to make it not an issue, you could genuinely stop this.

You can fake some benefits but can't fake a dopamine detox. Be still and go about doing the thing that hurts. Being mindful of your perspectives is vital.

Chapter 7:
The Dopamine Detox

When I tell people they have to go on a dopamine detox, they tend to think that I want them to be completely miserable for a few weeks. That's because their current interpretation of dopamine isn't exactly accurate. So, I want to start this chapter by sharing a couple of fun facts about dopamine. The science and psychology behind dopamine aren't always appealing to most, but I believe after reading this chapter you will want to learn even more.

After explaining and discussing what dopamine is, I'll share how one gets addicted to dopamine and activities that induce high levels of dopamine into your system.

Fun Facts about Dopamine

- Dopamine is always present.
- Dopamine has four functions: pleasure, movement, motivation, and inhibiting prolactin release.
- Dopamine doesn't work on its own.
- Some activities increase dopamine more than others.

- When you like something, it increases the dopamine that gets released during that activity.
- Drugs and supplements can't sustain dopamine.
- You can increase dopamine naturally.

Dopamine is Always Present

Neuroscientist Dr. Andrew Huberman says that people often talk about dopamine 'hits' as if there is a period in which dopamine doesn't exist. He explains that dopamine is always present in your brain. You have a baseline or natural level of dopamine, and some people's baselines are higher than others. This is why you'd find that some people appear to be full of life, and others are all gloomy. Your baseline levels of dopamine affect your overall temperament.

It is possible, however, for your dopamine levels to drop below baseline, or to increase above it. This is what's known as a tonic and phasic dopamine release.

So, say you're playing your favorite sport: Your dopamine levels are likely to rise above baseline, or the phasic release. After the game - or even after you've been playing for too long - your brain then decreases the dopamine below baseline, or tonic release, so that you can eventually get back to baseline. This is why after doing certain activities you feel drained, and not exactly motivated to do much thereafter, you just want to relax, maybe even sleep.

Dopamine's Four Functions

Dopamine is released along four pathways, which have four separate, but interconnected functions.

The mesolimbic pathway is what's responsible for the pleasure and reward function of dopamine.

These aren't terms you have to take much note of. Just understand that certain activities release dopamine and encourage you to want more of it, even if they're not good for you.

Next is the mesocortical pathway which releases dopamine from the VTA to the prefrontal cortex (PFC), which is what's responsible for motivation, drive, cravings, and committing activities into memory. There are certain activities that we would want to do for the sake of doing them, and not necessarily to receive pleasure once it's done. For now, remember that dopamine is what drives us to want to accomplish certain goals.

The nigrostriatal pathway is involved in controlling movement. If you have any movement disorders, no matter how subtle, you may find that your dopamine levels and therefore motivation is low too. I'd advise you to seek some medical advice in this case and see if you can treat or manage the underlying cause.

Then finally, the tuberoinfundibular pathway releases dopamine from parts of the hypothalamus to the pituitary gland, and thus inhibits the release of prolactin. So, whereas the release of prolactin would say you're full or don't need sex, dopamine release would have the opposite effect - therefore, both chemicals can't be released simultaneously. I want you to recognize that dopamine plays a role in a lot of different functions within your body, and isn't just about getting you stimulated and feeling happy.

Dopamine Is a Neuromodulator

Previously, dopamine was classified as a neurotransmitter, and if you were to look through most search engines, you'd find scientific resources that still define it as such. But it is a neuromodulator. Although it's released slowly into the brain unlike other chemicals, the effects of dopamine are very broad, and it can have an impact on many different cells at the same time. Huberman also mentions that it can affect how those cells express themselves and make changes to gene expression. Because it has so many roles, it makes sense that dopamine is always accompanied by other chemicals in the brain.

Activities That Increase Dopamine

Some activities increase dopamine more than others. This explains why we choose to engage in certain behaviors and not others. In his YouTube video, Huberman shares some activities that increase your dopamine levels high above the baseline:

- Exercise produces a dopamine high of up to 200% if you enjoy it. If you don't it won't increase the dopamine in your system at all.
- Sex (both the pursuit thereof and the action itself) produces a 200% increase in dopamine.

This might explain some of your behaviors or that of the people you know. These activities are highly addictive and can result in severe consequences like overeating and becoming overweight, sex and pornography addictions, as well as drug abuse. We erroneously link the good feeling to the activity itself, not the release of dopamine. This applies to all dopamine-inducing activities, even if the phasic level isn't that high above baseline. It's important to note here that you can choose to have a dopaminergic response to the activities that will push your life forward.

You Can Increase Dopamine with Fun Activities

When you enjoy something, you tend to do it over and over and find yourself talking about it more. This exercise of talking and repeating increases dopamine levels, and this can happen with any activity you choose whether that's playing video games or writing a novel. Whereas most of the activities listed above typically have a dopaminergic effect on almost everyone, certain activities are more subjective. This again, explains why some people would find gaming captivating, while others see it as a waste of time.

There are several reasons why you may find yourself only doing activities that you enjoy, but can't seem to do things that could be beneficial to your future.

Firstly, if you don't find the idea of making money through cryptocurrency exciting, even though it's a lucrative business idea that others enjoy, you'll always find yourself procrastinating when you're supposed to learn about Bitcoin. A potential solution here is to seek out the things you enjoy, and engage with these consistently.

Now, you can't lie to yourself and say that you enjoy something when deep down you don't, in this case, your actions will speak louder than your words.

Secondly, there's only so much you can spend your dopamine on. Dopamine runs out, and if you spend most of your time watching funny YouTube videos, you'll find that you're happy enough, and won't be motivated to now go out and seek more. Think of dopamine as mental cash, when you spend it carelessly when the time comes to invest in serious things, your wallet will be empty, and you have to wait until you make more cash. The problem is, we only ever remember how fun it was to spend our mental cash on unimportant things, so every time we do get more 'money' we spend it carelessly again, and it becomes a sad and vicious cycle, keeping us trapped in.

A third problem we face relates to the tonic and phasic releases of dopamine. So, let's say you do start working on a goal. After you achieve that first milestone (for example, doing thorough research on what is needed), you might feel really good about yourself, and you experience high levels of dopamine. As your brain attempts to regulate itself, your dopamine levels drop below baseline. Most people don't take well to this drop, and often try all sorts of activities (sometimes even supplements or drugs) to bring their dopamine levels back up.

Drugs and Supplements Can't Sustain Dopamine

Let's say you do feel somewhat better after drinking an energy drink, munching on some chocolate, or listening to music. It will most likely not be an instant improvement in mood - and you need to remember that some activities, like listening to music, can also increase serotonin levels which is another neurotransmitter that affects your mood. Be careful that you don't mistake small changes in your mood as directly corresponding to the activity itself.

Regardless of the intensity of the drugs or activities you do, dopamine is a self-sustained chemical. A better option for you is to just wait for your dopamine to reach its normal levels naturally.

Dopamine Can Increase Naturally

After dopamine has been depleted and drops below baseline, it will take a couple of hours, perhaps days if the dopamine peak was extremely high, for your levels to return to normal, naturally. You don't have to try and boost dopamine levels by engaging in activities or consuming anything to get your drive back up, in fact doing so can cause you more harm. The more you try to increase your dopamine (especially with unhealthy habits), the more you're damaging the dopamine receptors. What tends to happen, according to Huberman, is that your baseline level of dopamine itself drops down, and it will require more and more effort on your part to get a sufficient amount of dopamine to feel satisfied.

This is why some people experience burnout. They're constantly seeking activities to make themselves feel like they're on top of everything, whereas their brains need a break. That normal, then high, then low pattern is what you naturally thrive on. You aren't supposed to be extremely happy at all times, and if you treat your brain well, you'll never feel completely low either. I'd also like to mention there are ways in which you can increase your baseline level of dopamine so your general mood is more upbeat and you feel more motivated naturally. I'll discuss this later in the book. For now, let's focus on the core of this chapter, the dopamine detox.

How Addiction Works

The primary purpose of the brain is to allow us as a species to survive and reproduce, part of that includes avoiding pain (and death) and seeking pleasure. Pleasure, from a primitive perspective, would mean going out and hunting for food (so we can eat, grow, and sustain our bodies). It could mean spotting a potentially dangerous animal and fighting it to the death if we recognize we're strong enough.

It might include dancing around a fire camp with a family who loves and supports us.

Life today is vastly different from what it used to be 10,000 years ago. We no longer have to seek or fight for anything, and our social lives even before 2020 hadn't been disrupted. Attaining pleasures from what would seem like the little things in life isn't possible for us, and we have to sort of find other ways to gain pleasure. Fortunately, and unfortunately, the world we live in has a wide range of pleasurable activities for us to engage in. From video games, to fast food restaurants; we can have everything we could ever possibly want just by tapping an object in the palm of our hands.

Most of the activities you're engaging with tend to release high amounts of dopamine into your brain. The idea of stopping that activity, subconsciously, makes you aware that once you stop you won't be as happy, and so your reaction, again subconsciously, is to do more. So, one episode turns into two or three, or four. Once a day turns into three times a day. Soon you find yourself unable to go through a day without engaging in that activity, and every time you're not, you're thinking about it.

Huberman says that the craving for something (as you're constantly thinking about it) causes your baseline levels of dopamine to drop. You believe that if you engage in that activity again - just one more round - you'll suddenly feel so much better. But because your dopamine has already dropped below baseline, unless something exciting happens in the new episode that is completely different from what had happened previously, chances are your dopamine levels won't increase that much, and may only get back to baseline. So, you start feeling like you normally do, and not "happier" as you intended. Yet, because you remember that the first time you engaged in that activity, you did feel extremely euphoric, you think that simply doing more will allow you to get that initial feeling back at some point.

There are a series of events that may follow this:

1. You'll only be able to experience pleasure when you're doing that particular activity, and you tend to lose interest in everything else.
2. You get to a point where that activity itself doesn't make you feel any pleasure (remember I touched on anhedonia in chapter one), and you feel somewhat depressed.
3. You start layering activities to try and increase your dopamine, like eating while watching TV.

4. You start searching for more extreme ways to get your dopamine peaks.

The problem is, nothing you do will ever get you to feel pleasure again, at least not in the same sense. In some extreme cases, people may seek therapy, start taking drugs or even commit suicide. Psychiatrist Anna Lembke explains that addiction isn't only about seeking pleasure, but also about avoiding the pain in our lives. Pain can show up in many ways: loneliness, depression, and being underwhelmed. She says that people with addictions are bored in their day-to-day routines and are seeking a way to get more exciting experiences:

[Life] is very boring, because all of our survival needs are met.

Then on the other spectrum, it's not that our lives are boring, but because we've got so many experiences easily available to us, most of which are exciting, nothing else that we do would be as exciting. Your administration job in a tiny office is not going to be exciting and meaningful if you're constantly being bombarded with bright and fascinating videos on TikTok. Starting a business (for most people) and having to learn a new set of skills isn't as rewarding as watching sports highlights. All of this, even the previous examples shared, can be corrected with a dopamine detox.

How a Dopamine Detox Works

A friend of mine happened to call me up one day. I could tell from the tone of his voice that something was wrong, so I dropped everything to go and see him. When I got to his place, he greeted me in his usual upbeat manner, and we sat down, each with a craft beer in hand. It took a minute or two before he got to the point of our meet-up. He began by telling me he's been feeling weird. "How weird?" I asked, and he explained he almost felt anxious all the time. But this was a new feeling for him and not something that he'd say he had always experienced. He went on to explain that this anxiety is interfering with his work, and sometimes even hobbies.

I asked a few follow-up questions, trying to get to the root of the problem. No one just develops anxiety out of nowhere, there's almost always a reason behind it, especially for someone like him. He was such a cheerful chap: outgoing, talkative, active; not the type of person you'd pin anxiety on. But yet, here we were, trying to put the pieces together. I finally asked the right question: if there was any particular event that would trigger his anxiety or make him feel more anxious? He said it was his phone.

After his local podcast had gained popularity, he found himself constantly on his phone, checking new messages, comments, and other engagements from his community. Most of it was positive, but he'd had a few trolls. He dealt with them fine, giving them a taste of their own medicine, and letting it go thereafter. But he never knew which type of message would show up next. Would he be fighting with someone he'd never even seen before, or would he be sending heart emojis? At first, his palms only started sweating when he needed to open his Instagram account. His heart would beat faster as he scrolled through the comments and on a good day, it felt really good. But on those few days when he received a negative comment, it ruined his whole day, and he could even be thinking about it days later.

It later progressed, and just holding his phone in his hands evoked those feelings of anxiety. He sometimes felt like he needed beer every time he would have to touch his phone - which was of course every hour of every day. I asked him if he had to be on Instagram every day, would he be able to do any work if he'd removed the app from his phone?

"No," he exclaimed, "my fans need to see me, that is how my podcast is growing."

Again, I asked if they needed to see him every day on Instagram, and if it wasn't at all possible that he continued with the podcast and his daily routines, and just cut out that one thing, which was stressing him out. He was hesitant, so I explained to him that it appears that he's become accustomed to the likes and positive feedback on Instagram and that he needed to detox from it.

"Detox?" he asked, "I'm not some junkie!"

I tried to explain to him that it's not about being an addict, but just that to get his mind right again, he needed to do a dopamine fast.

"A fast?" he wouldn't let me finish, "Do I look like I need to lose weight?"

He didn't. He was in the best physical shape anyone could be in. I knew I wasn't going to get anywhere with him, so I dropped the subject, made an excuse to leave, and was on my way.

On my ride back, I kept thinking about what other words or phrases could I have used to make him understand. I wanted to help, and I knew my idea was right, but that didn't matter if I wasn't getting my point across correctly. By the time I got home, he had sent me a text:

What would I have to do on this detox?

I was so relieved. People can only be helped if they're willing to put their ego aside and accept it. So, I sent him a long audio note explaining this.

How to Do a Dopamine Fast

Stay away from your phone for the next three weeks. You can explain to your Instagram community that you're taking a sabbatical or that you want to spend more fun time with your family, and want to be completely present with them. You'll still be doing the podcasts, but you'll respond to their messages and comments after three weeks. If it was just Instagram making you anxious, I would've said just delete the app, but because it has spilled over to the whole phone, I do want you to stay away from it, up to a point where it no longer triggers you.

You're not allowed to take a sneak peek (on your phone or PC). You can't substitute Instagram with another social media platform either. You need a clean break from social media and the positive affirmations that come along with it.

Finally, during the time you're on sabbatical, think about better ways to respond to the negative comments, if you even need to respond at all.

What's Happening in the Brain?

Not all hope is lost. Your brain, for the most part, is highly flexible, and - provided you haven't destroyed your dopamine receptors (which is possible in extreme cases) - you're able to bring yourself back to your normal baseline levels. When I advise people to go on a dopamine detox, their initial response is always confusion or fear. Partly because they don't understand what I mean, and for those who have a rough idea, they're afraid that the consequences of a detox will be damning and quite frankly painful.

Understandably so; you're bound to feel uncomfortable, restless, and maybe even depressed during your detox. But something amazing is happening in the brain, which will allow you to not only get you back to normal but may even help you experience a new kind of happiness - happiness for the simple things in life. According to life and business coach, Stefan James, a dopamine detox helps you experience the other pleasure-inducing neurotransmitters like oxytocin and serotonin. These are often masked by the overpowering effects of dopamine.

Oxytocin is stimulated when you form bonds and connections with other people, particularly in the real world - not just social media. Remember your addictions often want you to push other activities (and at times, people) away, and only do things that will stimulate dopamine. Through your dopamine detox, you'll naturally want to be around people, and feel loved and connected once more. If this doesn't happen naturally for you, I'd strongly encourage it, to get that dose of oxytocin.

Serotonin is a neurotransmitter that gets released through a calm sense of competition and accomplishment. According to Dr. Loretta Breuning, "natural selection produced a brain that rewards you with a good feeling when you gain an advantage" (2018). Dopamine and serotonin are quite similar in this sense, but dopamine gets released even from easy wins. Whereas serotonin does require you to work a little harder. As you detox from your quick wins, you'll now be able to seek more ambitious goals.

Checking In

I checked in on my friend after about a week of starting the dopamine detox. He explained how he so badly wanted to reach for his phone, and at times had even forgotten that he was on detox and tried to look for it. Realizing a few seconds later, that it's safely locked in his closet. His life felt empty, especially in those "Instagram-worthy moments" when he'd have the perfect picture or video to share with his community, and couldn't do so. He wasn't used to living just for the sake of living and had gotten so accustomed to sharing his life with his online family, hearing their thoughts and opinions, and looking forward to positive feedback.

I knew he wasn't the type of person to quit, but I just reminded him to stick it out, and that he will feel a lot better soon enough. Sure enough, he did.

He called me with two days left in his three weeks and asked if it was possible to extend the detox. He couldn't believe how much he was missing out on in the lives of his real family. His wife and three-year-old were surprisingly funny. He was even planning on making a new baby. He explained that he didn't feel as bothered by those negative comments. Whereas in the first few days of the detox he still felt angry and couldn't imagine responding to them any differently than he had done before. Now, he feels so much empathy for them, understanding that they're getting their dopamine high by firing him up. He would no longer allow that. He went on for about a month and a half without his phone and decided he'll switch it back on, and only spend an hour on Instagram a day, focusing on sharing his experiences for the sake of sharing and growing his podcast, not necessarily to get positive comments.

A willingness to try and an openness to the experience are all that's needed to help you get the same result. In the next chapter, I'll break down some of the top behaviors people get addicted to and share why then how you should detox from them.

Chapter 8:
Dopamine Reset

A dopamine detox is more about allowing your dopamine receptors to reset themselves so that your baseline levels of dopamine return to normal - and so you don't impulsively do things that make you happy by sacrificing all the other areas of your life that require attention too. Constantly engaging in highly pleasurable behavior allows us to put a large plaster over a wound that's gorged open and in need of serious stitches. The plaster covers the open cut, but that doesn't mean it doesn't exist. We can only deal with the wound and all the pain involved in getting it stitched up by removing the plaster.

A Two-Day Break

Even if you aren't necessarily addicted to some of the behaviors mentioned above, I would suggest that you take a two-day break (or even a couple of hours a day) from certain activities. You can switch your phone off for a weekend retreat with friends and family. The urge to take pictures of yourself having fun will be a bit difficult, but if you collectively decide to keep your phones at home, you may even learn more about each other.

You can also do intermittent fasting for several days where you don't eat any food, let alone processed foods, for certain hours of the day. Many people eat from the minute they wake up to the minute they sleep. Perhaps you're not obese or overweight, but you may find this practice beneficial. Start by not eating for 12 consecutive hours per day, then push it to 14, then 16, and when you're feeling strong enough, 20 hours.

Taking Back Control

An old friend of mine sent me a message on Facebook. He was in Seattle and wanted to meet up. I was keen, I hadn't seen him in over six years, and you know, life can get in the way sometimes, and we just stopped communicating. No fights, and no trouble; we just didn't have anything to share with all the distance., we met up at a local pub, which sold the most amazing burgers - I mean thick, juicy, and savory - and after he ordered, I mentioned that I'd pass on that and just have a beer.

"Are you on a diet?" he asked jokingly.

I laughed and explained that I wasn't, but I just choose to eat at certain times, and also don't eat as many burgers anymore - I'm careful not to use words like "junk food" or "highly-processed food" in front of others because I don't want anyone to feel like I'm judging them.

He asked me how I did it. He had heard of intermittent fasting, but could never get himself to do it. It's like once he starts eating, he just keeps going on until he calls it a night. I briefly mentioned that foods like burgers can do that, but changed the subject because I didn't want our meet-up to turn into a health lecture.

We spoke for a while, his food came, and he offered me a bite, I declined, of course, and we had a good catch-up session. He told me he felt crappy and will need more beer, which he ordered. At this point, I said I'm good for drinks, and he asked if it was part of my intermittent fasting rules.

"Not really," I responded, but more that I wanted to limit my alcohol.

"Okay, what's your secret," he asked, "are you taking some supplements?" There were these protein shakes that were making the rounds, which helped suppress one's appetite; he thought perhaps I could be taking those.

I, again, responded no. He paused and gave me that look that said: "go on, please share," so I did.

The whole phenomenon puzzled him, but I could tell he was interested in the possibilities of what it meant if it was all true, and he could do it as well. We eventually spoke about other things, and he told me he was flying back to

New York in two days, but we should keep in touch. I had a good feeling that keeping in touch would include me talking about the dopamine detox and how I'm able to control my behavior by moderating it and finding ways to live my life in the present.

He has used the same principles in his life and says that he has never felt more in control of his emotions and actions. Before, he never understood his impulses but always had a feeling something wasn't up to par. He's one of those individuals that had a pretty decent life before doing the dopamine detox, but after it, he has experienced more mental focus, greater control, and the ability to just say "no thanks" when something doesn't sit right at the moment.

Chapter 9:
Why Bad Habits are Hard to Break?

Addicts frequently require both highs and lows in life. Many people develop addictions because they become bored in their lives when there aren't enough challenges. Because addiction typically provides stimulation in their lives, they are restless and constantly seek it out. Give up feeling bad about your attention-seeking behavior. Recognize your attraction to strong stimuli. Attempt to pick them carefully rather than dwelling on the "bad" ones. Use your new problem-solving skills to help you push through the unpleasurable withdrawal symptoms you previously sought to numb with the drug you now have to avoid. When you learn to distract yourself from a former dopamine high, you no longer need it. Fight cravings by thinking about something else. You are just one decision away from being your old self again.

Learning how to take control of your mind and how to beat your dopamine addiction is the most powerful skill you will ever develop. However, it's not an easy skill to learn and it will take consistent practice.

What gets rewarded, gets repeated. To master your mind, you will create a craving to do the things that help you reach your goals. When you do those things, you will feel the pride of a job well done.

Almost everyone improves their level of creativity, productivity, and engagement in their daily lives. However, few gain a simple, lasting boost in their ability to think without isolating themselves from their environments and the people around them. The key is to become comfortable putting yourself in a context that allows you to think clearly and creatively. This can be done by being around a few people who share the same interests and challenges.

Chapter 10:
Phone Addiction

Smartphone Addiction

Smartphones are an important part of our lives, but they can be addictive like anything else. Most people would agree that we rely on our smartphones too much and use them for things that we really shouldn't. Constantly checking our phones has become the norm, even when we are in company and some societies no longer consider it ill-mannered.

When we're not using our phones, we're thinking about them. We can't stop ourselves from constantly checking for new notifications, messages, and emails. And when we're not using our phones, we feel anxious and lost without them. This is what addiction looks like.

Smartphone addiction isn't recognized as an official disorder, but it's a real problem. And it's only going to get worse as we become more and more reliant on our phones.

The Reality of Smartphone Addiction

Most people don't eventually think of themselves as being addicted to their smartphones. Some of the dangers of smartphone addiction include:

- Decreased Productivity: When we're constantly checking our phones, we're not getting things done. We're distracted, and our productivity suffers.
- Increased Stress: Checking our phones for new notifications causes us stress. We constantly feel the need to be connected, which causes a lot of anxiety.
- Damaged Relationships: We're spending less time with our friends and family because we're glued to our phones. This can damage relationships.
- Negative Effects on Mental Health: Smartphones can harm our mental health. We may experience anxiety, depression, and even psychosis.
- Physical Health Problems: Smartphones can also cause physical health problems. We're more likely to get sick because we're not getting enough sleep or exercise and are constantly stressed.
- Dangers While Driving: Smartphones can be dangerous while driving. We're more likely to get into accidents because we're not paying attention to the road.

How Smartphone Addiction Manifests

Smartphone addiction displays in different ways for different people. They may only check their phone a few times an hour, but the need to do it is overwhelming.

There are also different ways that people use their smartphones. Some people use their phones to stay connected with friends and family, while others use them to pass time. Some people use their phones to escape from reality. Smartphones provide a sense of comfort and escape for these people.

How to Overcome Smartphone Addiction

Once you realize that you're addicted to your smartphone, it's time to take action. Here are a few steps that you can take to overcome your addiction:

- Make Changes to Your Phone Habits: The first step is to change your phone habits. Try to limit the amount of time you spend on your phone and be more intentional about how you're using it.
- Disconnect from Your Phone: Another way to overcome your addiction is to disconnect from your phone. This means turning off your notifications, putting your phone away, and not using it when you're with friends and family.
- Find Other Ways to Connect: Instead of relying on your phone to stay connected with friends and family, find other ways to connect. Spend time talking to them in person or try a messaging app that allows you to have group chats.

- Find Other Ways to Pass Time: If you're using your phone to pass time, find other ways to do that. Read a book, watch a movie, or go for a walk.

Can a Dopamine Fast at Any Point Quick Fix Your Cell Phone Addiction

Many individuals are looking for ways of getting away from vices that outcome in a reaction that doesn't feel better, whether it be depression or gorging.

They won't find an all-out arrangement in dopamine fasting. However, Berridge noticed that it's one significant component of opposing allurement.

"Dopamine fasting is an incredible system," when it's not taken excessively far, for example, staying away from eye-to-eye connection. "It's simply not the absolute arrangement," he said.

As a matter of fact, concentrating on the best way to effectively oppose enticement has tracked down that having a substantial methodology, such as seeing the treat plate at a party and deciding to stroll past and stand away from the desserts, is exceptionally powerful.

We can't simply request that the world disappear and not entice us any longer," Berridge brought up.

In reality, managing allurements or pessimistic sentiments or ways of behaving is not the same as the dopamine quick. To do this, Berridge suggested rehearsing care.

Care can assist you with concocting ways of managing troublesome things you'll experience day to day, while as yet appreciating daily existence.

To rehearse care, the following time you regard yourself as exhausted and go after your telephone to look at web-based entertainment thoughtlessly, delay, and observe what you're thinking and how your body feels. Then pick another thing to do all things being equal, similar to going for a stroll or making tea.

What Should You Do During the Detox?

The only thing you're permitted to do all day ... Please read my book ... Okay, actually ... So, you've cut the frivolous stuff and are ready for your hard reset. What should you do if you are fasting? My days are usually filled with walking, light exercise, and meditation.

The science behind dopamine fasting

So, can dopamine "fasting" help your mind? Specialists say perhaps, yet not for the reasons individuals might think.

Having some time off from an invigorating action (or every one of them) will quit turning on the dopamine framework again and again as regular daily existence does, yet it won't reset it.

Attempting to reset dopamine levels to build delight might rest on a misconception of how dopamine functions in any case.

Many years prior, dopamine was believed to be the joy synthetic. Be that as it may, specialists currently comprehend how it works — and its subtleties — all the more profoundly.

Dopamine is better perceived just like a substance in the mind connected with inspiration - and subsequently a significant piece of examining habit treatment - yet it's a touch more perplexing than that. It's important for a bigger prize framework in our cerebrum.

Rewards are things we both like and need

"The enjoying and needing of these things are independently relegated, and dopamine is liable for the needing," Berridge made sense of.

To separate this double framework, take the case of a text notification sound. You hear the sound go off, and you need to see what the text says. That is because the warning sound has set off dopamine. The message probably won't be a message that gives you joy.

"These [social media] signals are ideal little triggers for dopamine frameworks - regardless of whether we're preferring these things," Berridge noted.

While getting a hit of dopamine with another text can fortify, as per Berridge, it tends to occupy and upsetting if it goes excessively far.

Assuming that you feel attracted by virtual entertainment, which "consistently retriggers a condition of want," or one more wellspring of steady dopamine, he said that it's justifiable to need to remove yourself or get away from the source.

If consumed in excess, it may play a role in:

- Mania
- Hallucinations
- Delusions

Too much dopamine may contribute to:

- Obesity
- Addiction
- Schizophrenia

Parkinson's disease is characterized by tremors, delayed mobility, and, in some cases, insanity.

Over-activation also affects dopamine receptors, causing you to lose interest in other things. This can lead to more compulsive behavior. You're losing your ability to avoid utilizing these substances.

Addiction occurs when you consume more of a need than the desired amount. Even if you've been refraining from narcotics for a long time, being exposed to them may reawaken your desire and put you at risk of relapsing.

Dopamine is not completely to blame for the emergence of addiction.

Chapter 11:
Establishing New Habits

Settling for less is living lesser than you're truly worth. And the majority of us are settling for less. We are living far lesser than we are truly worth. Why? Because we've made ourselves believe that we can't have what we deserve and have gotten fed up with trying without making any headway.

After all, nothing is going to work out for you unless and until you are prepared to put up the required effort to make it happen. You will not observe any genuine good growth or change in your life unless you are the one who initiates and facilitates authentic good development or change in your life. For those of us who are concerned that we are not being provided with chances, and that we are being excluded from our country's economic potential, allow me to pose the following question to you: if an opportunity presented itself right now, would you be in a position to take advantage of it? Do you think you'll be employable in your current position? Do you wish to make a career change? In such case, what assets do you have that you may put to good use to make a reasonable income and provide for yourself in later life?

In life, everything is structured in such a way that it can only take place at a certain time of year and during a specific season. Remove yourself from the situation for a moment and ask yourself if what you're doing now will be able to keep you going for the amount of time you want it to and give you comfort in your life. If you haven't done so before, this is a terrific moment to start. Determine whether or not the things you're doing right now make you feel good about yourself and happy with your accomplishments by taking stock of your present position. It's important to ask yourself this question, regardless of whether you are happy in your life or just trying to get by (survive) from day to day.

Maybe some of us lack support; maybe the system is in some way working against us; maybe our community or neighborhoods are not inspiring us enough, or maybe your color is making you be discriminated against. I don't care what your excuse is for not aiming and exerting effort to improve yourself; I simply want you to know that "you don't have an excuse!"

If you make wonderful decisions and engage in extraordinary activities, you can't live a life that is not pleasant as a consequence of your efforts. Because we picked the easy way out of a tough circumstance, rather than because we lacked better options or because we ran out of better alternatives, "less" has become the defining characteristic of our life. As a consequence, we are making up justifications for not putting out the work required to live the sort of life that we want.

As a result, we begin to place the blame for our arduous existence of struggle and agony on everyone and everything else, other than ourselves. Because of your low social status, you will continue to suffer as a consequence of your failure to accept responsibility for your actions. You must live your life in the manner which you feel is best for you and your circumstances. Understanding your life's pieces and sewing them together into a coherent whole is your duty and task.

In contrast, you have a total commitment to yourself in every way; there is no one or anything else who is completely committed to you. Only if you want it and are willing to put up the significant work required to achieve your goals will you be able to live a fulfilling life.

It follows from the fact that you have total control over your circumstances that you can design an absolutely beautiful life ... As a result, I'd like to put the following question to you: "Are you content with doing what everyone else is doing, or are you motivated to achieve the highest possible level of quality?"

Chapter 12:
Ways to Naturally Boost Dopamine

Dopamine is the brain's pleasure, motivation, and reward chemical messenger. One can become tolerant to the amount of dopamine they are producing, directly causing them to not feel the effects of dopamine as much as they should or want to. Sometimes, people can then look elsewhere, like drugs, to find the dopamine they need to feel happy. There are ways to naturally raise dopamine levels without the need for opioids even if you feel like you're lacking dopamine highs without them.

Your dopamine detox will include the things below. You don't have to do all of them, though. You can pick and choose the ones you will stick with for the duration of your detox. The more of these things you can add to the list, the better. While they might sound extremely hard for now, you will have the fantastic experience of replenishing your dopamine receptors later on. Keep in mind that your detox can be the turning point of your life. The type of things you can do to detox your dopamine receptors will depend on your individual life and what you usually do when you go seeking dopamine.

As long as the person continues to use the addictive substance, the brain adapts to this situation and gets used to it. To normalize fluctuating dopamine levels, it reduces its natural production of dopamine and lowers the number of receptors and areas of the brain that dopamine stimulates. Therefore, the addicted person starts to use more drugs to bring the dopamine level to "normal", which we call tolerance.

When dopamine is released, the environment that you're in is etched into your memory and stays there for a long time. For example, if you see your friend, whom you used to drink alcohol with, or a bar you went, to years ago, you may suddenly have a craving for alcohol. As a result, even if you complete addiction treatment, the environment you live in may remind you of your old life.

There are some ways to start rebuilding your dopamine receptors safely and naturally. Maintaining a safe level is up to you and is very important. You can try some of the methods below after your detox to slowly introduce healthy behaviors for dopamine production.

Consume Protein-rich Foods

You can fill this deficiency by consuming plenty of protein-rich amino acids, specifically one that increases the level of dopamine, and tyrosine. Examples of foods rich in tyrosine are beef, eggs, milk, legumes, and soy.

Reduce Consumption of Foods Containing Saturated Fat

Foods containing saturated fat, such as butter, whole milk, and coconut oil, have a property that disrupts dopamine signals in the brain. Therefore, you need to consume these foods as little as possible.

Eat Prebiotic Foods

Bacteria living in the intestines directly contribute to the production of dopamine. Consuming foods like probiotic yogurt that support this production and are also good for mental health can help. There are a lot of flavors and types of prebiotics available in grocery stores these days. Kefir, yogurt, kombucha, and kimchi are all widely available in stores.

Exercise Regularly

It has been proven by scientific studies that aerobic exercises are effective in the treatment of Parkinson's disease (Oliveira de Carvalho et al., 2018). By taking at least

30-minute walks a day and exercising, you can avoid diseases that are caused by a lack of dopamine.

Get a Generous Amount of Sunlight

Especially in the winter months, people who don't get enough sunlight may experience mood disorders. You may have heard the term "seasonal depression." Fresh air and the boost of vitamin D will make you feel the effects of dopamine. However, you should avoid sun exposure between 10 a.m. and 2 p.m. as the UV rays might be dangerous.

Vitamins and Minerals

You can increase the amount of dopamine you produce by taking magnesium, iron, folate, and/or vitamin B6 supplements. At the same time, you can eliminate a dopamine deficiency by consuming 2 cups of green tea a day. However, before you start using vitamin supplements, you should have a blood test and consult a doctor, especially if you are a recovering addict or taking medication.

Chapter 13:
Controlling Your Dopamine for Motivation, Focus, and Satisfaction

After removing compulsive diversion, what comes next is: What to do in reality when detoxing from dopamine? Well, rushing toward something is simpler than running away from it. You will probably relapse if you don't create a more fulfilling life without the internet and if you don't work to address the root causes of obsessive technology use. In little time at all, you'll return to your unhealthy behaviors. What do I mean by a more fulfilling life? You might do things that will make you feel good such as dopamine detoxifying exercises which include; speaking with others, eating and cooking, taking a walk, acquiring books, journaling, and exercising.

You'll see that these hobbies all move you away from screens, which is something they share in common with. Additionally, these are all illustrations of what I mean by seeking high-quality leisure. Describe in detail how you can use your time more effectively. Think about it: What are some simple tasks you could perform if you start to feel a little bored? It could be drawing, fishing, rock climbing, journaling, reading, or tidying your space. Additionally, now is an excellent time to do some exploring. Enroll in a salsa dance class, start an origami project, or pick up the flute. Make an interest that has previously been inactive, active.

How to Take Part in Actual Activities

List improved go-to activities

Making a concrete list of these activities is beneficial. When you peek at a physical list that is posted on your door or refrigerator throughout the day, it will serve as a reminder of productive ways to fill your time. Every time you take a quick look at that list, you're reminded that there are more productive ways to spend your time than checking social media or watching pointless YouTube videos.

1. Phone or default actions

Distractions are still present, but you have additional methods and resources at your disposal to help you manage them.

2. Environment design and context cues

The list is a context prompt from a behavioral perspective something in your environment that directs you to do a certain action. You see the list (the actual item), you see the suggestion to "tidy up," and you begin tidying (action). Note: if you enjoy organizing things, this is a simple task for you. Something else could work better for you. Choose tasks that you can perform even when you lack motivation. Of course, you can utilize other kinds of context cues as well. Example: Normally, you keep your phone next to your bed on a nightstand. You probably don't want to approach the day in this manner. Change the way your environment is designed instead. Purchase a manual alarm clock or move your phone away from your bed so you have to get out of bed to silence the alarm and place a book on your nightstand that you want to read (this is the context prompt for reading).

By doing this, you can increase the likelihood that you'll read a few pages of a book to start the day off well rather than scrolling. A book on the nightstand, a pair of jogging shoes by the door, a list of one to four things to do when you have nothing to do; all of these context cues in your immediate environment will help you remember what you had planned to accomplish., what do you want to do when you start to get a little bored? What would you like to do that you wouldn't later regret? Create a tangible list right now. Despite distractions, maintain your focus. Get a useful newsletter with blog entries, quick suggestions, and illustrations about avoiding procrastination. Do you have questions like what will I do all day if I quit browsing the internet mindlessly?

Perhaps you've spent so much time "online" that you don't know what to do when you're not. As we've discussed here, engaging in high-quality leisure activities not only makes you feel better but also helps you improve your life by giving you a stronger sense of who you are. Instead of aimlessly consuming entertainment like social media, Netflix, or video games, use this checklist of activities to unwind. Although it may appear completely mundane to some, this is exactly how I felt at the time. I recognized my life was empty and had nothing but work when I tried to substitute the low-reward pursuits. I was unable to focus on my thoughts at that time. I numbed myself with the cheap dopamine so I wouldn't have to face the difficult choices I had to make. So, although it's not ideal, I frequently tried to work extra. Burnout can result from not allowing you enough time to unwind. A condition in which one would forgo anything work-related and spend days on end partaking in cheap dopamine-producing activities.

When you are having trouble concentrating Take a stroll and discover the local nature or your neighborhood. Tired? Take a nap or, if it's nighttime, go to bed early (read this if you're having trouble doing so). Overwhelmed? Take out a piece of paper and a pen, and begin recording your thoughts. It can just be your feelings towards a particular subject or all the things you have to complete. When you start worrying about something and begin to put it on paper, the issue frequently crystallizes and is quickly solved.

Moving in any fashion not only improves the health of your body but also your mental clarity and resiliency. Remember, even one time a week is preferable to none. Your choice of activity will rely on your interests. Simple walking is acceptable. Go outside if you have easy access to it. Take a hike, or take a bicycle. If you're not an elite athlete, exercise should mostly be enjoyable. You do it more frequently if it's enjoyable for you. You become in better shape and start to feel better if you do it more frequently. If you don't enjoy going to the gym, you are not required to. Try practicing martial arts, yoga, swimming, or various sports. When there is no work to be done, learning can be the perfect pass time. There are three key areas you can concentrate on:

Develop yourself

Start a journal and ponder life's big questions, visit interesting places, meet interesting people for coffee, or look for new experiences.

Read

Books exist on just about anything. Some are humorous, others instructive, and still others are philosophical. Choose the genre that you are most likely to stick with. Your horizons can be expanded through reading in a variety of ways. Find a marketable skill to learn (design, programming, copywriting, foreign language, or a trade skill). Check to see if you can find an engaging online course on any particular subject.

Food

We eat every day, so knowing more about the topic is very useful. Either learn to cook or develop your cooking abilities. You could, for instance: Learn to prepare meals in advance. You'll spend less money and eat better as a result. Learn the fundamentals of cooking; Get into food fermentation by making your kimchi and pickles. (As a side note, fermented foods are very healthy for us.) Start baking; make pies, cookies, brownies, or sourdough bread if you want to eat healthily. There are countless options. If you have the space, invite friends over to cook with them or for them.

Almost everything mentioned above has to do with taking action, creating something, or learning how to create something, as you may have noticed. We don't want to imply that engaging in entertainment is always undesirable. Some of it is top-notch entertainment. The issue arises when things go wrong and we overindulge, are unable to control our behavior, and neglect all other obligations. We refer to it as the compulsivity risk. The following are some factors that lower the risk of compulsivity:

- Playing board games in person with other players
- Reading or hearing books on tape
- Consuming a quality podcast

Visiting a theater or a movie: Going to the movies is an event with a set start and end (plus 15 minutes for commercials). The likelihood of binge-watching movies at the theater is low because one must get dressed and go out.

Going to a museum, gallery, zoo, etc.

All of the aforementioned choices are of a high caliber, but what if they are unappealing or overly costly? Do your usual cheap dopamine activities in that case, but only if you can do them in person and with someone else. Generally, following this rule will ensure that you don't overconsume and that you'll interact with the person:

View a program or a film.

Join a friend to play a video game.

View a sporting event

There is a sense of genuine social connection that many of us lack these days when there is another person present. Find a more effective way to fill the void. These are some doable and practical ways to pass the time, so there you have it. They might require a little more work, but they will certainly be more rewarding than mindlessly scrolling through your phone. We cannot work continuously. We must unwind. But how we go about it matters. Pick leisure pursuits wisely. Despite distractions, maintain your focus. The activities listed above might not occupy the bulk of your free time, so you should pick up any hobbies you abandoned or never began due to the internet, such as playing musical instruments, drawing, etc. "I've always wanted to do ____, but I never had the chance or the time." You will have the time if you detox off dopamine.

Chapter 14:
Proven Ways to STOP Being Lazy

STOP Procrastination

Procrastination is a common stumbling block. Dickens referred to it as the "thief of time." Is it possible to manipulate our brains into undertaking difficult and unpleasant things?

Why do we procrastinate?

First, we must find out the cause of procrastination. There are biological reasons for procrastination, it turns out. It's not all our fault.

The limbic system is just concerned with what feels pleasant. It naturally avoids unfavorable situations. It's unconcerned with deadlines or long-term effects.

Your prefrontal cortex, on the other hand, serves as your organizer.

Dopamine Detox

This involves depriving your brain of dopamine for an extended period. Because the brain seeks stimulation and simple rewards when that dopamine rush is removed, even difficult, monotonous, and necessary jobs can appear enjoyable.

All you have to do is avoid dopamine-rich activities such as Netflix, internet or phone surfing, sweet foods, booze, and so on. Unplugging from dopamine has been found in studies to improve mental attention and clarity.

Develop a Timeline in Detail

Have you ever noticed how you are more inclined to procrastinate when a) the project is vast and difficult, and b) you only have one deadline that is far away? A single chore can easily become overwhelming, especially if it's painful.

Instead, consider breaking things down into small steps and assigning a strict deadline for each step. Begin small to gain momentum.

Collaborate With Others

It's much simpler to slack off when you're not accountable to anyone else or no one is keeping track of your progress.

This person must be focused and diligent, as well as unlikely to slack off. For example, your best office buddy may not be the best anti-procrastination weapon. There are even virtual coworking applications to help you remain on track these days.

Remove Distractions

The majority of individuals procrastinate because they are preoccupied. If you lack the discipline to resist these diversions (see: dopamine detox), you can at least reduce their impact. Place your phone in a different room.

Try internet filtering programs such as Freedom and Forest. Close the actual door or find a quiet place away from people and conversation.

Reward Yourself

In psychology, the standard habit loop is trigger, behavior, and reward. The job we don't want to do is the trigger for our procrastination. The behavior is to avoid that work (which feels good ... to a point). And the reward is a relief, which, predictably, does not last long.

Mindfulness

Mindfulness assists us in breaking free from the trigger-reward feedback cycle by allowing us to connect with our emotions: curiosity, the delight of accomplishing good work, and the anxiety and stress that typically accompany procrastination.

Chapter 15:
How to Make Hard Work SUPER EASY

Develop Optimism

Optimism can become a self-fulfilling prophecy. Running the mile in less than four minutes was considered a physiological impossibility, almost like exceeding the speed of light is thought to be a physical impossibility. Thus, no one was very optimistic about achieving this goal, and no one was able to do it. But then one cockeyed optimist named Roger Bannister refused to accept that limit and went on to run the mile in 3 minutes and 59 seconds. Interestingly, once the myth was broken and it became possible to imagine beating the four-minute mile, an entire succession of runners soon broke the barrier.

The pessimism that we carry with us is often due to messages we've received from others, such as a teacher who told us that we can't learn math, or in the case of the four-minute mile, a societal assumption. When we internalize these messages, they become "deceptive brain messages," a term used by psychologist Jeffrey Schwartz, who demonstrated that we can free ourselves from these pessimisms by realizing that they come from other people and are not our own true beliefs about ourselves.

Studies show that in addition to helping us achieve goals, optimism increases happiness and other positive moods, reduces anxiety and depression, enhances the ability to cope with negative situations, improves physical health, and results in other benefits.

What can we do to become more optimistic? One proven practice recommended by positive psychologist Sonja Lyubomirsky is to keep a diary, in which we write down exactly what our future will be like assuming we have achieved all our important goals in the various areas of life - career, relationships, spirituality, and so on.

Writing and repeating positive affirmations is another good way to cultivate optimism. Optimistic affirmations can be repeated at specific times during the day, such as when we're falling asleep or after we just wake up. Or, we can repeat them to replace negative thinking whenever we become aware of it. According to positive psychologist Tal Ben-Shahar, affirmations about achieving future goals are more effective if we intentionally recall our past successes, which provides encouragement and evidence to back up our positive statements

Pursue Your Own Goals

Here I'd like to present three basic principles that research in positive psychology has added to the vast literature on setting and pursuing goals.

1. Setting and pursuing significant goals is one of the main sources of human happiness.
2. There is at least as much happiness, and possibly more, in pursuing a goal as in achieving a goal. As American philosopher Horace Kallen said, "The going is the goal."
3. Pursuing a goal, results in much more happiness when it's our own goal - a satisfying and meaningful goal that is closely aligned with our interests and desires—rather than a goal that we feel compelled to achieve. Our goal might be to climb a Himalayan peak, build our own house, learn jewelry making, find shelter for homeless people, teach computer literacy in a third-world country, or almost anything.

In an experiment at a rest home, a group of residents who were allowed to make many of their own choices about their activities demonstrated significantly more happiness and health than a group for whom most decisions were made and almost everything was done.

Goals that are not our own would of course include goals chosen by other people that we pursue out of obligation or guilt. As Steve Jobs said in his 2005 Stanford commencement speech, "Your time is limited, so don't spend it living someone else's life ..."

Less obviously, goals that are not truly our own and have been shown to result in less satisfaction, also include goals that we pursue only for an external reward, such as money, fame, beauty, or power.

Of course, we might want or need to pursue a goal that's assigned to us by someone else, or a goal that's focused strictly on earning money or another external reward. Positive psychology has simply shown that those goals, however necessary they might be, don't result in as much happiness as goals that are truly our own. So, we can boost our well-being by adding a few of our own cherished goals to our other life aims. We might pursue these personal goals during vacations or other free time.

Conclusion

When you learn to avoid highly stimulating activities that destroy your ability to remain calm and focused, you'll find yourself capable of tackling your major tasks with more ease than ever before. Going through a dopamine detox will help you lower your level of stimulation and ensure you work on your major tasks.

It's safe to conclude that our understanding and study of the long-term impacts of technology are very restricted.

As individuals get older and more accustomed to social media and wireless technologies, further discoveries that alter our interaction with the digital world are likely. Obesity and screen time were found to be positively associated in a large study of over 90,000 people, independent of physical activity.

A longitudinal study found that excessive television viewing was responsible for 60% of the overweight incidence in their study.

Our vision also affects our physical well-being. According to a growing body of studies, around half of the population will suffer from Digital Eye Strain (DES). DES is a syndrome that causes symptoms such as aching, dry, weary, burning, or itching eyes, headaches, sore neck, and difficulty keeping your eyes open. It is undeniably treatable, but no research has shown the long-term influence on our vision.

This not only affects our sleep, but it may also create certain health problems, as circadian rhythm abnormalities have been linked to cancer, metabolism problems, and cognitive dysfunctions.

Because sleep is a major difficulty for many individuals, there is a chapter dedicated to providing you with advice on how to enhance your nighttime routine and obtain more sleep every night. So, stop letting your environment hijack your brain and regain control of it instead.

Author's Note

Dear reader,

I hope you enjoyed my book.

Please don't forget to toss up a quick review on amazon, I will personally read it! Positive or negative, I'm grateful for all feedback.

Reviews are so helpful for self-published authors and your feedback can make such a difference for my book!

Thanks very much for your time, and I look forward to hearing from you soon.

Sincerely,

Gary

Made in the USA
Middletown, DE
16 December 2022